WE ARE MERMAIDS

Also by Stephanie Burt

Poetry

For All Mutants (chapbook)
After Callimachus
Advice from the Lights
All-Season Stephanie (chapbook)
Belmont
*Why I Am Not a Toddler and Other Poems by Cooper Bennett Burt,
    Age One* (chapbook)
Parallel Play
Popular Music

Literary Criticism

Don't Read Poetry: A Book about How to Read Poems
The Poem Is You: 60 Contemporary American Poems and How to Read Them
From There: Some Thoughts on Poetry and Place
The Art of the Sonnet (with David Mikics)
Close Calls with Nonsense: Reading New Poetry
The Forms of Youth: Twentieth-Century Poetry and Adolescence
Randall Jarrell and His Age

Edited Collections and Editions

The Cambridge History of American Poetry (with Alfred Bendixen)
Something Understood: Essays and Poetry for Helen Vendler
    (with Nick Halpern)
Randall Jarrell on W. H. Auden (with Hannah Brooks-Motl)

WE ARE MERMAIDS

Poems

Stephanie Burt

Graywolf Press

This publication is made possible, in part, by the voters of Minnesota through a Minnesota State Arts Board Operating Support grant, thanks to a legislative appropriation from the arts and cultural heritage fund. Significant support has also been provided by the McKnight Foundation, the Lannan Foundation, the Amazon Literary Partnership, and other generous contributions from foundations, corporations, and individuals. To these organizations and individuals we offer our heartfelt thanks.

Published by Graywolf Press
212 Third Avenue North, Suite 485
Minneapolis, Minnesota 55401

www.graywolfpress.org

Published in the United States of America

ISBN 978-1-64445-205-9 (paperback)
ISBN 978-1-64445-188-5 (ebook)

2 4 6 8 9 7 5 3 1
First Graywolf Printing, 2022

Library of Congress Control Number: 2022930743

Cover design: Kapo Ng

Cover illustration: Sam Chung @ A-Men Project

—for all the letters in our alphabet, and the people inside them—

CONTENTS

A surprising thing has just happened at the Abbey, about 2 months ago a young man called Carter came and joined, he was very pretty and very effeminate looking. He told Monck, that he sometimes went about in girl's clothes, that his family in order to make him manly had sent him to sea but that it was no good, he has run away and now they had consented to his going on the Stage. Monck hated him with a sort of blind fury, and did everything to get rid of him because of his feminine airs. I found that I had a shrinking from him, and noticed that the men generally shared it, at the same time I felt the pathos of the poor boy's life, for he was obviously always trying to ingratiate himself with everybody. He didn't re-join this term, he had an aunt and begged various members of the Company if they met his Aunt not to mention him. Last night in the Green Room a member of the Company told us all how he met the Aunt and the Aunt said "my niece tells me she has had such a pleasant time in the Abbey Company." The result was universal fury, the angriest of all was a young woman who said that he or she had tried to put his arms round her waist. I understand that he or she is now dancing as a woman in the Pantomime! He or she as a young woman would have been perfectly charming.

—W. B. Yeats to Lady Gregory (21 January 1912)

I took his face in my hands; it was terribly urgent that he understand. "How am I to fit back into myself, after this?"

He laughed softly. "Haven't you always been more than yourself? We are none of us just one thing."

—Rachel Hartman, *Shadow Scale*

Beneath the city is another city, where everything matches us.

—Jane Yeh, *Discipline*

We Are Mermaids

The salt of the ocean is always the salt of tears,
melancholy but at the right
dilution, or concentration, life-giving.

It has been there since before
the beginning of tragedy,
when what would become
us was just trying to get through the day.

We know the consistent waves, as they
ride fortune's helical gears,
sacrificing their poise for their careers,
need not be the only mode of living.

Look down: the thermophiles
sip at the fumaroles,
whose sulfur steam would kill a human being.
They love it here. And the mottled, diffident ray-
finned fish known as zoarchids or eelpout,
all shrugs and S curves, choose
to nose along the floor of the rough world.

They are both predators and prey,
with gills and wide-set eyes instead of a face.

You don't have to be use-
ful. You are not required
to come up with something to say.

You can spend your life benthic, or brackish,
subsisting and even thriving where a fingertip
comes away saline and still refreshing,
exploring the estuary, the submerged lip

and congeries of overlapping shores
on the green-black water, the harbor, the bay.

You can live with your doubt,
that's why it's yours.

Some of us are going to be okay.

"   "

We have a soft spot for drama,
        and for memorization;

we like to share whatever we have been told.
        We liken ourselves to tadpoles, to works-in-progress,

to fishhooks, to earbuds, to loquacious
        teens, and to their vintage Princess phones.

We used to believe that, being so good
        at belatedness, we might never have to get old,

which was our mission, or our curse;
        though our true age is unclear, we have had equivalents

in nearly every civilization,
        both in our efforts at sarcasm and our attempts
at protests. Leave our single sisters alone.

We come in several shapes but are never
        heartless, or pointless, and never entirely straight.

If you ever see just one of us,
        wait.

Miami

Not the sense of standing alone
in front of a microphone,
but the adjustments of playing along
with a more experienced band.

Not the fear of representing
an establishment, but of representing it badly,
of being inundated and then shipped home.

The scallops whose breathing
tubes pop up
above the receding salt water,
through the overlaps of sand.

The fear you'll sink like a skipped stone.

The past, as it grows
away from you, is thickening.

The young reader in the too-often-washed
Avengers T-shirt with the collar cut out had asked,
"How do you deal with the fear of existing?"

The insubstantial feeling
that came to you then, the vertigo,
and the quickening.

Potomac River, 1982

where I grew up
it was all wonderful and
defensive

the adults were kind
and never neglectful
bringing fresh water and

grapes oranges and juice
and sunscreen always asking
each kid what we would

need or might need in the
anticipated future with its
goldenrod-bordered

cleared field
its soft blacktop
its estimated yield

we were told to look up
with reason to keep
looking forward

to a cloudless sky
punctuated by drones

you had to hide
to be alone

Cabbage Whites

When we were caterpillars we
were meant to be left and could be left
amid our claque of leaves, each on our own.

We spent our lives in search
of sugar and cellulose, or shelter and shade.

Now we live out in the open, protected,
if at all, by our apparent
insignificance, or by the speed
with which we pivot and change direction.

We know we are nothing much
to see beside our brighter, nobler cousins,
fritillary, viceroy, swallowtail:
eye-catching, exuberant, tansy and coreopsis,
flower-on-flower beside our favorite weeds.

And yet we believe
it is better for us to be
this way than any other, better to be
what looks like pallid shyness from above
or from the perspective of color photography
but honestly comes to us as continual effort,
a matter of learning our ultraviolet
signatures, of willingness to fail
or else get lost in loops, jumps, lacy spin.

We may not have much longer
to find one another. We do expect to be found.
At least we know where to begin.
We got along once

without eyes, without wings, under eaves, on the unfrozen ground.
No danger, no inclement
weather, no stalking or
aerial predator
can make us choose to live that way again.

Boeing 757s, Airbus 320s, an Embraer 190

We were made to do this:
to wait indefinitely,
to make sure we are in tip-top,
polished shape and cleared
of frost and other obstructions
before we take off,
to get a specified number of human beings
wherever they think they are going, to be
at once mulishly on task and hyperresponsive
to nuance, to the right statistics' direction
regarding turbulence, gravity, convection
or freezing rain, whose apparent
shellacking we may shrug off
with not much more
than a bump, a flap, a chemical wash, a cough.

We are aware
that we have younger cousins,
some of whom face mortal danger
if we were to come into contact, skin to skin.
We like to believe we have
no wish to be like them.
We look out at them from above, from our serving-
plate-sized windows, our dozens of wide-lidded eyes.
We do not confide in them. We put on an act.
Each of us plans
to honor our contract.

We can accumulate ice, or get
alarmingly hot underneath.
In sunlight, our fuselages shine like candy,
the kind that can break your teeth.

All of us grew up
in places that look just like this,
except for the weather. Some are so far away
tomorrow there starts halfway through today.

Our first law, or command-
ment, is not to harm
these bipeds who rely on us, who would be strand-
ed otherwise. Though we know they can fit into land-
bound vehicles with tires like ours, we suspect
their sort can't go without our sort.
We do not believe that any of them can leave
their single, fenced-in, assigned-at-assembly airport.

My friends and I have invented—
better to say discovered—a kind of religion,
according to which we are dragons,
voluntarily (our sect has it)
taking into ourselves this diminutive, fragile
but also (as we now know) sentient species
with almost no hide, two eyes,
and thin, vestigial wings,
a species that needs our help just to get in the air.
In return they feed us, and let us
breathe fire, for only as long
as we can keep them all safely up there.

Another denomination, however, has it
that we are really in captivity,
that we have been ensorcelled, that the bars
and primary colors along our spines and tails
have made us forget who we are, that we are not meant
for passengers but for unaided,
unlimited trips around the troposphere,
singing and signaling only to one another,

and that we remain on the ground
in obedient geometrical formations,
queued up and preoccupied, out of habit,
having determined that we ought to follow
other parties' specifications,
their aging grids and literal guy-wires,
out of an excess of caution; due to the memory
of long-ago collisions; out of respect
for our elderly, who suffer from metal fatigue
and hope to be put on display once they retire;
for our difficult sisters, who require
spot-welders and wrenches always
at the ready, who cannot take another dent;
or else out of our even simpler fears
of the unknown, or of abandonment.

My 1993

I lived in a closet. Also I lived in a closet
Belonging to my then-best friend's then-beau

Who lived with three other men in a Central Square
Walk-up, spacious and sunlit, except

For the closet. The closet abutted Horace's bedroom
(Horace is like, but not quite, his real name).

Horace lived as a rent boy for a B-school professor.
The others did—I never knew what they did,

That is, "consulting." I was proud to be the new
Coat-check girl at a cavernous bowling alley

Recently made over into a cavernous rock club.
I was working for tips. I wanted to say

I was working. Really I was playing
At self-sufficiency. Mostly I was playing

Records nobody else liked for two hours a night,
Or four if the next DJ never showed up. I liked

To pretend that other people were listening.
Sometimes they called me up. I felt at home

Where no one could see me. I liked the Verlaines
And Treepeople, Small Factory, Circus Lupus

And Some Velvet Sidewalk, the Dead C and the Spinanes,
Who sang about thirsty anomie in a voice

Like sour cherries, sweet with overtones
Of sharp and ripe and bloodstain. When I moved out

I lost two crates along with a cardboard box
Of 25 ten-year-old vinyl LPs I took home

(Home meaning the closet) when the former guitarist
Was throwing them away: wrapped, black-and-white,

With a picture of an angry toddler running.
Their most famous song was about not being

Famous, not being in school or employed, just "hanging
Out in the Boston rock scene." The band was called

Sorry. They broke up before
I could see them. The album was called *Imaginary Friend*.

At the Parkway Deli

You can know what you need before you know why.
For example, ten-year-old me, who leans
on the empty, cold salad-bar cart along the cold wall
of the crowded dining room at the best Jewish deli
(supposedly, though they're not kosher) south of Manhattan:
I'm waiting for noon, when the cart
becomes the world-famous pick-your-own-pickle bar.
"World-famous," meaning
I wouldn't stop telling my dad how much I liked it:
green sour tomatoes that pop
whenever you cut or bite into them,
intricate as a satellite inside;
sauerkraut in three colors, like some nation's flag
left outdoors in a storm and shredded, maroon,
not-quite-white and pale emerald-green;
half-sours and dills, sliced lengthwise like canoes,
curled up at their tips like canoes;
banana peppers the shape
of your tongue if you stick out your tongue,
that also burn your tongue;
jade disks with peppercorns, sugary like tart candy,
yet not dessert, and good for you. How many years
till I found out why trans girls and women crave salt.
Coming out makes your blood pressure go down.
So do spironolactone, and other
similar shots and pills with jawbreaker names
I wanted to change me. I would tell no one.
I would stand outside until I was 41,
waiting to be let in. You can know what you need
before you know why: shredded cabbage and mini-cukes
and sodium ions in water, and vine-ripe tomatoes
preserved in mustard seeds, coriander, allspice
and vinegar for no one knows how long.

Impatiens

Montgomery County, Maryland

Petals that flourish in shade,
the deeper the better; they treat
the sun much as we treat the sun—a friend,

as long we don't have to see his face.

Indigo, moth-wing, beetle-carapace blue.

They were the single flower or flower name
that stuck in my mind
after our mother decided we ought to try gardening
together: my brothers and I
needed to get dirt on our grade-school hands.

The resulting muddy fingerprints
were temporarily everywhere indoors.

The mature blooms can lay across
each other casually,
like couples in high school hallways,
or else in late middle age;

once settled in their shallow
excavations and properly sheltered
from overexposure, they
can almost be left alone.

An uninformed visitor, seeing the shapes
they make in their raised wooden beds,
could take them for pansies,
although they are more resistant

to winter, and never display
anything like a "face."

No matter what choices you make
you will entertain second thoughts.
You could always have run away,
or grown some other way.

Who did you want to be, before you knew
who you were going to be, today?

Hobbies

In the Holly Hobbie board game (Parker Brothers, 1976), you move your dime-shaped token over squares around a brick-walled wishing well and try to guess secret wishes.

Each secret wish has its own card.

The cards have rounded edges, like standard playing cards scaled down to fit young hands.

Their style is what you might call extreme Laura Ashley: gathered caps, phlox, ruffles, Queen Anne's lace, wicker and gingham, puppies with floppy oversize ears, penny-farthing bicycles.

Each time a player guesses another player's secret wish, the player who guessed correctly can take from the well, or rather from the stack at the square border of the well, one, two, or three pennies.

The "pennies" are cardstock discs in lemon yellow, the size and shape of a real-life dime. Holly has worked hard to save them, but we know she does not need to earn a living. That's what makes her Holly Hobbie.

You can use pennies to buy your own wish.

Some wishes are a Letter, a Swing, a Parade. Other wishes are a Birthday Party, a Beach Day, a Horse, and My Own Desk.

None of the wishes involve survival, or safety, or ambition, or competition.

You can also wish for a Best Friend.

Each player represents a different child: one has fine blond hair, another black curls in ribbons. One wears a romper, another a smock dress. Two wear overalls.

Not all the children are white, though the board is.

The adults are out of the picture, perhaps at work, or taking care of younger children.

The only disappointment comes on the face of the cat on the card whose wish is Lots of Kittens; she looks sad to see the eponymous basket of kittens (one black, two orange, the rest mottled or striped) taken from her by a girl (Holly Hobbie) who has trouble lifting them all.

Holly will feed them all milk, slowly, from her glass bottle.

You can pay with pennies for answers to any question, as long as the answer belongs in the game.

The back of each card shows a figure in pastels: a child in a mob cap, a plaid dress, and spring-weight boots, holding sprigs of mallows (the flower, not the dessert).

Each card repeats a slogan in art nouveau font:

> *Red, Yellow, Green and Blue,*
> *May Your Wishes All Come True.*

Thank you, cocreator or uncredited maker of work for hire. Yours too.

My 1994

I didn't know. But I knew. I took off the dress
Kay offered and apologized for my striped boxers.

I called myself a kid in a candy store
When I was a teen in a lingerie store. I wanted

To move to a place I knew secondhand, from TV,
To Topshop, Boots, postcodes in England-land. I had mixed up

The opposite of nostalgia—a longing to be
Some place I could never call home—with my wish

To become someone new. There's a wasp between
My windowpane and its wire-mesh screen. She wants

To get out. She hovers and dives toward some
Way, not knowing there can be no

Way unless someone unlocks the glass and lifts
The window itself and lets the wasp into the room.

For *you* read *me*. I wanted to write a book and I told
Everybody I knew that I wanted to write a book

About the softest pop groups I could find:
The boys wore striped sailor shirts and they sang

Like girls and the girls wore striped sailor dresses and sang
Like every first kiss was simultaneously

The Holy Grail and no big deal, which was true
And is true. The Field Mice. Heavenly. Blueboy. I loved

Them all. I love them all. The demand that we shed
Our previous selves is garbage. We are not wasps

And need not leave our shells behind. I had
To move to England to see them where they lived.

You say love could break a boy's heart,
Keith Girdler sang. *I said there's no such thing.*

I wore the sailor shirts but not the floppy collars.
My then-best friend gave me bad advice about passing,

Telling me women dress for one another.
Never for ourselves. My then-girlfriend needed

To date a boy. I was glad to help her find one.
I didn't know. But I knew. Maybe everyone did.

The wasp rams the glass, black and gold. I thought I wanted
To free myself from my body, which was

Not possible. Land
On this windowsill with me.

In Memory of Keith Girdler

I never craved endless summer. I still want an ever-
       lasting spring,
with all the beach roses, all closed in their buds, and weeds,
       where nothing has had time to fall apart.
If I can't recover
       that child in her one pose by the undemanding sea
on the cover of your first album, on that severe-
       ly foreshortened strand, where the salt recedes
over and over and the twelve-string
       acoustic guitar
works hard to reassure,
       then let me be
your mermaid—no, your jellyfish, buoyed and protected (oh spray,
       oh echo) with no desire
to grow or leave the water near the shore,
       whose ghost-clouds swell and sink, and stay almost clear
where sunlight divides the shallows, light making a loop
       like the *e* in the not-yet-popular word *transgender*,
the spinning glint on a vinyl record,
       the rounded *q* in the word *queer*.

Hymn to Youth

after Jaime Gil de Biedma

Where did you go—no, where are you going,
where do you want to go, years
that made up my youth, however you count yourself now?
Who will take you back to the beach?
Remember how calm the grownups remained, palms
open, grasping their pencils and pens and their purses
lightly in their left hands, when they should have known
we would hurt ourselves. We hurt ourselves.
We rumbled through our own imaginations
as in the middens of clothes at Dollar-a-Pound,
trying on gowns, capes, suits that never fit.

You were the waves. We could live among the waves,
arising and lapping and falling back, salty and pure
like the salt inside us. Our little breasts,
our half-curves, our ambitious, ambiguous bodies.
You in particular were all insinuations,
muscular hints I was never meant to take.
Afternoon sun made a temporary
mirror out of the last, lenticular sand.
Our footprints left stiff slots for future tears,
the kind the sea brings everyone.

We were becoming. We brought you. You kept us there
in search of crests and troughs, anywhere we could leap
and dive and overwhelm our bodies,
looking for conch shells, clam shards, far fins, dolphins,
ways to call out to those other youth undersea,
who blew their triton notes and called to us.
They were the capacious luxury
of this life, imagined as another life,
more intense, more free. (Look: I've changed my style

from a one-piece to a two-piece, with scalloped
briefs and fluffy ruffles. Want to see?)
You didn't want us so much as we wanted
you, sophisticated starlet
with the manners of a yawning lanternfish
or the timidity of a just-crowned prince.
When we lost one friend we knew
we would never find another. We never did.

Salt hurt the bottoms of our feet.

They said we would be kings
if only we learned to hold hands . . .

You were never one thing, my youth.
You were a terror, a missed chance, a come-again,
a kind of eternal return. When you come to my door,
today, far from the sea, I let you in.
Sometimes you are Daphne, tormented
by that insistent, obtuse pursuer, the sun,
and sometimes you strike a pose,
indifferent, like Antinoüs,
to what I want, to what anyone wants,
content to be seen after hiding, among the men
and women, the training bras and the just-in-case shorts,
the outgrown rain slickers and broken-in running shoes,
the closets full of night and nonbinary angels,
the selkies, the griffins, the Fair Folk who taught you to fly . . .

Come in. Sit down. I don't have a crown or a throne.
I do have an armchair, a plush one I found on the street
in August when the students were moving out.
There are things I want you to see,
now that I'm beautiful,
as you wanted to be.

( )

We, too, feel uneasy alone; we believe we exist
to keep you safe and self-contained, at the cost

of making you seem, or feel, like you might not matter,
or not from the outside,

or not much.
We try to protect you. We have nothing to hide.

We can adjust
ourselves to look straighter, or flatter,

or more like sharpened claws, but we largely prefer
the state in which we resemble finger-

nails, or a French manicure,
reaching out with both our hands, your cure

for shapelessness, for your persist-
ent feeling that you will forever

remain immaterial, that you are better
off that way, that there is nothing or

nobody you are ready to let yourself touch.

Prayer for Werewolves

Someone will probably love you for who you are.
    If not, you'll still find friends,
friends who, given time, or given warning,
    will probably gather around you, hold your hands,
and wrap you in soft coats and blankets till the violence
    inside your body ends.

Someone will probably love you for who you are,
    not just for who you labor to be.
Maybe you're lost in your skin today. Maybe you're burning
    and wish you could tear it all off. Please don't. You are variously
a marvel, an athlete, a wilderness, a source of warmth
    and a way to learn from fear.

When you have claws, your claws are yours, your ears
    bristle and are yours; your irises
are citrine, pure, and yours. They let you see
    through smog and pine thickets and into the future, where
you need no chains to feel secure,
    and someone will probably love you for who you are:

then you will know each other's scents
    and nuzzle or lope together. But for
now, you have friends,
    who are not going anywhere. Please
stay here.

Love Poem with Comic Books on Saturdays

(Greek Anthology 5:219)

It's better when you blush
        before you kiss me, better
if they don't find out.
        Let's tie each other's shoes.
Let's run a race we mean to lose.

        Let's have a crush
that violates the spirit, but never the letter
        of the Comics Code,
where what you almost
        see is more important than what you can.

Let's run together like melted butter
        under our shared cotton coverlet
tonight, and never let
        anyone tell us we're brave, or foolish, or bold,
nor give each other reason to doubt.
        Let's make each other toast
tomorrow morning. Get out your pocket
        calendar. Let's make our sleepover plan.

Cinderella

The trans story is the heroine has to be trans
because nobody else in the capital shares
her size. The prince must roam from house to house,
from mansion to cottage to townhome, trying to find
the one girl who came to the winter solstice ball
in glass slippers (they must have hurt like hell
by the end of the night, even rightly sized) with heels
at least 1½" high, and (more important)
in ladies' 13½. But the longer
trans story is the prince was already
kissing and sharing secrets with his footman:
raised as a boy, the prince's favorite footman
was really a girl named Cindy, but only the prince
knew her chosen name. They could never marry:
the kingdom wouldn't accept it. So he told
her. And he wouldn't want anyone else. So when
the king insisted he choose, at that ball, a bride,
the prince arranged for Cindy to show up, splendid
in tiara and heels, all starry like Andromeda
viewed from a moonless mountaintop. When
(the plan went) the king asked the prince the next day
"Who was that girl you spent the night with?" he'd tell
the king to scour the town for Cindy,
the one who got away. Except that Cindy
didn't get away: instead she arranged—
of course, of course, unbeknownst to him—
to pop out from a family friend's garage,
then pop the question. And the prince said, "Yes,
I've changed my mind; we're not going to hide anymore."
That's the version we give the cis, and it's lovely, but
the truth is almost nobody gets it right:
the trans story is that the prince herself
is the trans girl in the story, and like so

many of us, she spent day after day—
before the party, after the party, maybe
instead of attending the party—crossing the town,
ringing doorbells, trawling message boards, scouring yard sales
and barging into shopfronts right before closing
to talk to the tired clerks, never giving up
her search for the one, the terrific, the just-right shoe.

Love Poem with Archery

It's like touching without touching,
except when there is, also, touching.

We pull the bowstrings back
and parallel together,
aiming a handsbreadth higher
than we believe we intend,
and let the glove move where we draw the wire,

scared that the machinery
will misinterpret us,
that we may not stop trembling, that we may lose
our belief in ourselves
before anything is released, or shared, or sent.

And yet we trust the nock to know
the whereabouts of the bow,
and trust the tail or fletching
of each salvo to astonish
the target as soon as it gets there, to make its point
within its nest of Os and Os and Os.

Our belts and buckles try to keep the secrets
we have begun to decide
that, later, we want to expose.

There is the rest of our group, and there is the river,
and that is called the kisser, the stabilizer
on your shoulder. Do what I do. You have time.
Put your hand over my hand. That feels nice.

No longer too young
to participate in this activity, we have become
the elevated counselors
of the air, which will not take
anything but our gentlest advice.

Love Poem with Summer Camp Reunion

Either the rest of the world
is camp, with bunk beds and splinters and firewood
and challenging, never-silent mattresses,
or camp is the world, on the day we were all dismissed
to our cabins, given the pummeling rain,

the day we locked toes, and knees, and learned to believe
that we could actually exist.

Do I want to be with her? Or do I
want to be her? As if our fingertips
had always been touching, as if the nervous connection
between us ran up our spines, and into our brains.

It was like
manifesting a tail,
like being able to see
a face that could see me, a face that would stay
with me through the as-if-predawn,
warm lakeshore-foam-and-moss-colored mist.

She is already on her way,
with all that long-delayed physicality,
ropy muscles, the ribs you can touch, and
flowers. Cones of flowers. Nearly uncountable,
multiplied, uncrumpled-wrapping-paper
flowers, rosemary and baby's breath and a central array
of roses, like the center or the bud
we could feel together through cotton, through the uncountable, tiny
mechanically printed flowers
on the wireless (as in telegraph), underwireless bra
of the first girl I . . . the only girl I . . .

And there she will be, across the jetway.

Is there any way to expect,
or just to be able to say,
how the anticipation is as exciting
as anything I can imagine that we might
let ourselves do, tonight
or at least today?

Before the Wedding

(Sappho 31)

That man you're standing next to . . . For so long
I looked up to him like a god. You're immured in conversation
And when he smiles back at you now, my heart
Skips, and not for him.

Tonight I need armor to look at you; when I want
To tell you how we should be together, no human
Language comes out. I have known this feeling
That warms, then scalds, me

Before, when you and I touch: it's the best
And the worst—I'm brittle tin, I'm paler than drought grass,
I shake, my eyes turn black, and I can't see you
Anymore, and yet

I do. I am going to survive this experience
Even if it's like coming back from the dead. Still, I wish
I could be taking your hand now, even if my
Horns and tail would show.

Let's go upstairs for a minute and look at the moon.

Song of Kate the Pirate Queen

I used to be the most relatable gifted child the world had ever seen,
in my Yoda sleep shirts and pointe shoes. Come at me: I'd take it.
I used to be everyone's sweetheart. Now I'm a brass-buckled, leather-booted
 pirate queen.

I used to hold newcomers' hands. We could hit the mall if you were sad, and if
 you were mean
we could fix that with ice skates, cocoa and pie. I'd bake it.
I used to be the most relatable gifted child the world had ever seen,

though I preferred circuits to circle skirts. You could sit me in front of any
 cathode-ray terminal, console, futuristic machine
or robo-Nimrod, and I'd neutralize, rewire, reprogram or remake it.
I used to be everyone's go-to girl for tech support. Now I'm a scarlet pirate queen.

I was the acceptable face of the unaccepted, sweet politic gaze on a screen
proving any of us was like anybody else, because I had taught myself to fake it.
I used to be the winsomest wide-eyed gifted child the world had ever seen.

I stayed in school till I could run the school, and strangers still believed I was fifteen.
I still like equations and costume closets, but now I love my sloop and the hungry
 wake it
leaves on the froth of the open ocean, now that I'm an implacable privateer queen.

If growing up means dying, I've died, and then some. I came back sharp, crisp
 and clean.
I'm trusting enough you can fool me once. I'd rather ignore a barrier than break it.
I used to be everyone's confidante, pert first crush, best friend, transparent like
 you've never seen.
I used to be responsibility. Now I'm your bare-knuckle, blades-drawn, power-
 politics bisexual pirate queen.

Some Like It Hot

Maybe it's better to stick with slapstick.
Not that you get to pick. When, in the famous
last minutes, Jack Lemmon flips off
his wig and tosses it, hard,
into his other hand, he means
to keep it. But when Lemmon-as-Jerry-as-Daphne
brings himself to admit,
despairingly, wryly, wonderfully, "I'm a man!"
to Joe E. Brown, who wants to marry him,
he is a man;
otherwise there would be no joke.
He will never not be a man.
He just can't help it. So that when Brown,
delightedly, gleefully, confidently, announces
"Nobody's
perfect," he could be
telling the world that he's gay,
or bi, or demi, or pan,
as the kids now say.
He lisps. He flounces. Look at his flappy hands.
He too is a man, in a way,
or maybe a boy, invulnerable to shame.
He doesn't even know Jack Lemmon's real name.
The braid and anchor on his hat
might almost be a golden scallop shell,
a token in what Jerry calls "the old shell game."
Meanwhile, Tony Curtis has proven able to redeem—
it's apparently every red-blooded straight bloke's
wet, or anyway ocean-adjacent, dream—
the studiously, deliberately, self-protectively
ditzy Marilyn Monroe,
aka Sugar Kane, who also believes—albeit
for better reasons—that she's found

a partner who fits her Miami Beach demands,
one who can play—so to speak—in the same band.
You have to believe it to see it. We would like you
to write about *Some Like It Hot*,
said (and I gladly accepted) the commission,
not because you are hot, but because it's a classic
someone like you must know, or understand.
It is, like Jack Lemmon's, a compromised position.
The waves stroke the bay and the sun slaps the lens and Jack
Lemmon mouths something unintelligible
even to modern lip-
reading experts as credits roll and we see money
is the real subject of the film:
if you have enough you can do what you want.
Everyone else will keep laughing at you,
but only behind your back.
Money is what makes you eligible,
and "eligible," of course, means you have a choice.
Traveling musicians, raconteurs, professionals fluent
in body language, oboe, or trombone,
my advice is don't get clocked;
come out of your (as it were) shell.
Go ahead and tell them who you are
before you lose your nerve, or your follow spot, or your voice.
So many people will want you to know
that they didn't know (did they know?) and now don't care.
Would you rather they show
you they're shocked,
their eyes happy saucers of wanting, as if you
had told them you
were the Shell Oil heir?

Frozen Is the Most Trans Movie Ever

because it was snowing in our transparent hearts
for 100 minutes or 40 years

and because the ancient rocks
while well-intentioned have big ears

they are older than Satan and bent on finding a hero
and a leading lady and singing to them

till they make a perfect match
for every lady they believe there exists a perfect catch

because the deleted scene is the chaste male lead
pretending to be a fisherman

from mysterious lands because fractal isn't a word
other princesses know because we learned it in math

we were afraid our parents would be canceled
in postproduction for shame for the gods' own wrath

because the presexual is so much like the postsexual
or the post-compulsory-heterosexual

because life on earth depends on the anomalous fact
that liquid water contracts while ice expands

because what matters the most
or maybe just what matters first

is not who you kiss or want to kiss
but where you let yourself hold hands

Introduction to Trans Literature

> If later on you want to read a good novel it may describe how a young boy
> and girl sit together and watch the rain falling. They talk about themselves
> and the pages of the book describe what their innermost little thoughts
> are. This is what is called literature. But you will never be able to appreci-
> ate that if in comic-book fashion you expect that at any minute someone
> will appear and pitch them out of the window.
>
> —Fredric Wertham, *Seduction of the Innocent*

> Comics is a form about visual presence, a succession of forms, that is stippled
> with absence, in the frame-gutter sequence.
>
> —Hillary Chute, *Why Comics?*

A young boy falling and a young girl in the rain
are together in a fashion. Their little thoughts
pitch through them like the rain, and at any minute
they expect someone you will never
appreciate. This is what is called young. The rain
keeps pitching down the gutters, against the selves
the boy rubs between inner windows, talking about
the presence in their little wants, and the innermost rain
you will never be able to describe:
you may never be a girl, but you can be good
if a novel in fashion describes you. Later, you appear.
The boy and the girl want to describe themselves.
Instead they expect that some literature will appear
to rain them out of the window. Their pages
describe. You can't pitch the rain. They can only want
to appear in the book of themselves, and if they sit
together they may call a window. Rain talks
to the gutters. The falling boy, who may be a girl,
may never be out till later, but the girl's book
will be good, it will be a comic book,
it may be a boy and a boy and a girl together,

a girl and a rain boy and their innermost girl,
whose pitch is falling together, so they are all able
to be young. No one pages them. No one appears
to pitch them out in the rain, or into the gutter
they may later appreciate. There will be pictures
of frames together, and falling, and stippled minutes,
and comic-book windows, and pages about themselves,
and this, this—this is what is called literature.

—

I'm proud of my work,
if you can call it work:

I am, also, fond
of far-off lightning, and completed connections,

and *and* and *and* and *and* and *and*.
I want to be everyone's long-distance friend,

a second-chance source for anyone's tenuous spark.
Like sex, I may be overemphasized,

overlooked and misused, kept out of the most polite quarter.
No mark I make should ever

be final. I love the idea of public performance,
like a girl on a wheel in a spotlight on a wire.

I see myself as neither straight nor curved.
And yet I am all too familiar with

the experience of creativity as temptation,
the feeling that you are always required

to volley, that you are never allowed to serve.
Every tragedian I know is a liar:

the announced end of a story is never
the end. That postcredits scene is my salvation,

my first line of self-defense,
the board I break, the myth I use against myth.

I am insatiable, forever
and always still swimming, and on my way. I take

and wonder whether I give. I know what it's like
to believe you have an appeal you never deserved.

Whale Watch

If you approach the surface
calmly and early enough
on a breezy day like today,

you might see them go by.
Long ago they would stay
for hours in their huge metallic

shells with fin-sized bolts,
some trailing chains as thick
as an estuary eel;

they would gather at the tip
of each shell, and all look out
as if to say goodbye

to a wave, or to a cloud,
or to ice, which your
great-aunt may still remember.

Now all their shells are made
from bones of fallen trees;
for steering and propulsion, they

carve branches, which they dip
into the sea, then pull back,
two at a time, like so.

Sometimes they grunt or hiss
while propelling themselves,
almost as we do when

we begin to grieve.
The woven grids they keep
affixed to the largest shells

work like baleen, although
much coarser: they secure
sea grapes, sea lettuce, kelp

and bladder wrack, the basis
of their diet, which they augment
with herring or capelin.

Take care not to swim too fast
or rise too close; some shells
flip over easily,

and their ability
to dive is surprisingly
limited, although

it varies considerably.
They cannot hurt us,
though long ago they could.

If you stay nearly silent
long enough, you might
be able to hear their chirps

and specks—a work song, perhaps,
or one of the greetings or
warnings they emit at the upper

limits of our hearing.
Your calves will likely have
more luck than you.

Snow

It used to settle on the crowns of trees
unevenly, so that gravity or a breeze
could make a fringe fall down,
the fluttering particles meeting their two-
dimensional shadows, off-
white occluding off-white.
Children could scoop it up

in disposable clear plastic cups
for later use, keeping it safe
in something called a freezer.
They would add sugar on top
or drops of harmless
coloring, so that the cup
would gradually turn red,

or green, or pink, or gold.
Left undisturbed, it softened
then over a night became ice,
and might crack under your foot,
or else support your weight,
if it had been cold long enough.
Sometimes it arrived

as early as October
and stayed here until February at least.
Deer used to leave
their tracks in it: little
divots, little less-
than-desperate explorers,
naive enough to be afraid of wolves.

Whiter

2017

Welcome to our America. It looks
the same as it did: snow, where it
came at all this year, melts earlier than ever
over shut union halls, tin diners, big-box stores
five miles out of town, where ever-brighter

arclights trace twin tracks that never
meet: shut trains and double yellow lines, two-, six-, eight-, four-
lane interstates all the way to the headquar-
ters of our gaslighter-

in-chief, where the Anacostia
disappears in the Potomac under the floor
of the labyrinthine, subterranean FDR

memorial.
If they met Lady Liberty they would indict her.

Whitman tacks into the wind, up the East River
and north by north toward an unknown shore.
The nation his peers wanted to cover

with fruit trees is a stack of apple cores,
a parade float of apple blossoms that might or

will rot in the snowmelt. Winter is already over.
What should have been shiny, stable, harmless, pure
enough for a harmless snowball fight or

sculptures when all schools are canceled hovers
as mist over slush, like the gray decor
favored by Whistler's mother: not *1984*

but 1876. The *gastarbeiter*
whose genuine war, whose flinch or fight-or-

flight response to the back of the hand
and the hand that feeds you will never get in the books.
Show us your papers. Make the handcuffs tighter.

America was America before
we tried to make it fairer, braver, brighter.
It seems, from above, very near
the same. But whiter.

Rain

The secrets decrease

There is no dust
to dust only
rivers and rivulets

their attendant
clouds and what
clouds let in
to the sea

The entire ache
the homeostasis
implicates you

If only you had face
and force and voice
enough to keep it off

better than bone
dry as a cough

It collects on glass
we broke
The continuing emergency
comfort us now

our wet yoke
our helplessness
on our good day

Anyway walk the dog
it's something to do

The earth needs something to do

Civilization

as in Boston
as what it looks like
when you leave it

taking off
your undercoat
of smog

as if from inside
the gumball machine
at the top of the old
control tower at Logan

from when we built airports
and thought they could stay
half the globe away
the President expostulates and is

no longer followed by
his opposite number his doom
his ghost his
Little Rocket Man

I'm not the man you think
I am at home
I am not he

nevertheless I wish to leave
this message for
civilization thanks
for everything

for feijoas also known
as pineapple guavas
multiple names
for all the best things

for César Franck's violin
sonata for fanfiction for
the next
generation

where nobody should have
to start from scratch
to start over

as if coming from
deep space or
deep water anyway *it feels
like we might have made it*
as one later singer

managed to say
we are not
going to be okay

Sparrows in the Natick Collection

I was not born
here. But it's here
that we feel safe. Above the near-
ly clear perpendicular rafters, each split sunbeam
apportions its angles over the bald spots, scarves, bedazzled
baseball caps, and effervescent water features four
stories under us, over the shadows a gaggle
of us throw down when we dive for
crumbs or popcorn
nibs. So   little we need.

Why do you
see me, if   you do see
me, not as a   reason to
look up, but as   a bother to be
removed?   What harm can I do?
I peck at your trash and may help
carry it off; I exemplify the proactive,
practically motivated hubbub and bustle
that you claim to want in the young. I am visible
but not heard: distracted
and nearly self-

        sufficient
introverts, I
   and mine never meant
       any trouble. We hide our eggs; we work the third
         shift half the time, and give your cleaners the harmless slip
         even before they know it . . . But now I think I've figured
        out what bugs you. We have seen you stretch flat rope
        to keep light-fingered teens away, or herd
          their older sisters out by
            closing time,
          and we know:
          you can stymie

our settlements, strike our camps, let loose an undertow or wave
    of borax, bleach or soap around our nests,
even poison our outdoor cousins; nevertheless
    we live here. Nothing you do can make us leave.

Turkeys in Harvard Yard

They don't belong, but who does?
Maybe their plan is to burn the whole place down.

Look at them directing the few pedestrians,
overruling stoplights. They have come to see

one another as heroes of distributive justice,
travelers from a pre-Columbian dawn.

Their ruffs rise up. Their collars make good fans,
their wattle-strewn beaks the vehicles

for once-presumed-impossible demands.
They remember when everything was icicles,

expensive gutters stacked with snow, their toes
on crusted ice the only sound.

Now they're our anti-fascists.
While we were limp in our beds,

sleep crusting our narrow lashes,
they had already taken control of the town.

Two Shields

(*Greek Anthology* 6:127-28)

1

I hated the fray.
      I couldn't wait to leave—as I have left—
the chaos of blade and lance
      and mud-caked boots and thin shaft after shaft
of futile, or snapped, or bloody arrows,
      piled up over young men who woke as the sun rose
but would not live out the day.
      What's the point of dying for renown?
The dead have less use than a pebble, a shell, a smooth stone.
      Now the girls who love Artemis dance
around my perfect bronze-bordered circumference,
      and the man who used to carry me, having grown
too old to fight, has thankfully come alone
      to her grove, said her prayer, and set me down.

2

Bright thing, sacred thing, accessory
      to the Great Man theory of history,
accoutrement of a conqueror who brought peace
      by ruling everything, enjoy your place
high up on the temple wall, with your polished trim.
      When you were Alexander's, your gold rim
was marbled with bits of soil, blood, pus, and bone.
      He would not leave the world alone,
and you had no choice. You had to accompany him.

Love Poem with Major Appliance

Though we could imagine circumstances far posher
than those of our lockdown, and others far more punk
rock—elbows flying, amps blown out, a mosher
in every corner—the banged-up cookie tray with trails of gunk
across its gray-green surface; the disgusting gusher
from the no-longer-hidden rubber hose; the funk
that suddenly filled the laundry room; the slosh, or
rather trickle, of clean water through that hose; the junk,
the literal nuts and bolts, fastened again, and the tools (potato masher?
aluminum snake? metal merfolk-tail?) back in the trunk
of home improvements, have left me in awe. Sure
of victory once the bin
begins to hum and spin,
you sashay downstairs, bowing like an ecstatic monk,
and sing to the whole of the house: "I fixed the washer."

?

Sligo town

This small child at a travellers' halting site
(in American: trailer park)
chose to arrange
two-dozen-odd slabs of cracked asphalt,
each about the size of a housecat,
so that
they made a straight path, then veered up to the property line
in the shape of a giant, crumbling question mark.
Anything, given time, can become a fine
art. Anything can turn over, or decline,
or break, or come back together, or simply change.
Put that in your model museum. Put that in your vault.

Lamb's Ear

No more at home here
     than the lambs, though no
        less so
     among the Banks Peninsula's steep,
        grassy, and almost pathless
declivities, the paired-off stalks can grow
     to the height of a house cat; they slouch,
        almost as much at ease
as a cat would be, amid the taller foxglove blooms, whose butter-popcorn and
        flame-orange bells emerge
so early in the Southern summer's game,
     as if to ring in the new year.

Too soft to be called teeth,
       too thick, except
     in direct sunlight, to see through,
the diminutive lobes on their immature
     aluminum-gray or Statue-of-Liberty-green
leaves' edge look faded even when brand-new.

Their paler fur will catch
     a drop from a hiker's water bottle if it spatters,
       if that hiker happens to slide
down the unexpectedly parabolic
     curve of a given hillside.
       Though dwarfed by nearby sheaves
of bladed flax, or harakeke, the wooly stems
     can hold their ground like hooves;
       the individual petioles try
to overtake one another, competing
     harmlessly, like teams
       in the fairest of sports.

Each puffed leaf-ridge seems to invite
        a child's finger and thumb.
                No thicker than the skin
of a tuned kettledrum,
        they might have come
here in search of a world without force,
        or at least without force of arms.

If they could speak
        they would not; they would wait
                for a durable peace,
        for people taking one another on faith
                across the continents,
as well as in this not-quite-wilderness
        with its traced-in, bush-sheltered not-quite-farms,
where no human being or sheep
                is likely to get entirely lost,
        given the tree-bark hash marks, dry plank
shelters, twine-bordered streambeds, and occasional hand-carved
        fenceposts with their hand-mounted
                scarlet or cherry-red fire alarms.

Geysers

Rotorua

Like photographs of tailings in Montana
turning cobalt-blue in mining pools—

No. This is something the earth did to itself,
catastrophe beauty, sublimity, condensation,

diminutive bubbles whose source no one can see.
They are the springs of human action,

pure until we get up close, or try
(but we can't) to see them from above,

sometimes surrounded, or obscured, by experts,
thick, rounded recent fences, and milled steel,

so we can view them safely now.
In the adjacent dissonance of the hot puddles,

effervescence rules; forever new,
forever ephemeral, mud-pool eyes and eyestalks

communicate incessantly with each other,
a language with no spoken or written form.

Do they know they won't last? Do they think they're failing?
Would it be better for us to have no feelings?

Kite Day, New Brighton

The color of soap on scuffed slate,
the beach can't rinse its suds off, nor get clean;
the eyes on the tallest box kites ask what it means
to feel you've come of age too late,
to crave, wherever you live, a change of scene.

Powdered sugar and cinnamon
under our toes and heels,
the seagulls choose expensive meals.
Surf approaches but never touches the fire-eaters
on their buskers' ziggurat of sticks and stones,
and the shallowest wash, in the heat of the day, still feels
too cold for wading. It conceals what it conceals.

Despite the alarming flapping sound,
a baby-blue manta-ray-
shaped, pickup-truck-sized construction
of parachute fabric contends
with itself; nearly spherical and improbably big,
a bubblegum-pink winged pig,

two fire-breathing dragons, a blue whale
and a square of colors inside colors glide
in parallel, so that they stay on the right side
of the spectator-safety exclusion zone.

The afterimages the kite strings leave
seem not so much serene
as optimistic, even blithe,
as if they could believe
a civilization were good for everyone.

The manta-ray kite, now fully deflated, maintains
a series of cuts along its sleeve.
Somebody's boom box settles into the end
of the Velvet Underground's "Who Loves the Sun,"
then shifts to the Verlaines.

Kurt Wagner's Song

after Paul Verlaine

The sky above all, with its acrobatic
Confidence, stays as blue as the sea,
As me.
Its sense of order is emphatic.

All three
Of us can hear the sweet church bell
And the jays repeating themselves. They are trying to tell
Us their divinity is real

And wants us to stand up for our real selves,
Once we know what they are.
My God is, also, real,
As real as humor and grief, as breakfast and elves,

As foil and épée.
Wind rolls lost chances off the roof.
The sky is ultramarine, and Prussian, and teal.
Blurred clouds extend their mesh of fur and lace

Above the soft earth like a circus tent
With a high-wire act: famous, dangerous, heaven-sent,
A definite maybe. A form of chivalry.
What will you do with your youth,
It wants to know, once you are safe
And free?

Bleeding Hearts

They do not fit their given name. They glow
all day in the sun, without
ever opening up; they are able to retain
their shape and their seal under even the weightiest rain.

They may assert, or believe, that any problem
they notice among themselves must be a low
priority next to the crocuses, always picked first,
or compared to the unwell maple, whose phantom limb,
as recently as last summer, could provide
an afternoon of unreliable shade.
Their practice at holding their own
has made them feel less cultivated or planted
than like something they themselves have made.

Nevertheless it is tough for them to remain
so sanguine; they have arranged
to keep themselves together in almost the same
way they keep other people's secrets,
even when shaky, at dawn, or nearly asleep.

They dangle and dodge in light wind
as if they were windchimes. They are, also, perennial,
able to outlast frost: they can insist
that the most important fact about them—more
than photosynthesis
or chromosomes, varietals or
Latin names—is just
that they continue to exist.

As well as the overfamiliar valentine,
the thumbnail spade for archaeological digs,
they duplicate the alphabet: a V

for victory, as well as a sort of X
wherever two or three will overlap.
Their bone-white, surprisingly durable
extensions resemble parentheses,
or quills, or claws. Once I heard
them claim that they were eggs,
dragon eggs; one day they would, supposedly, split,
detaching the bloom from the ornamental top,
so that the V-shaped part would drop
to Earth, and low-to-the-ground observers could see
the dragonets discover their feet,
their solarized scales, their yet-to-be-sharpened pairs
of retractable talons. The adults who share, or repeat,
these stories must be, not gardeners, but magicians,
the kind who understand how to escape
from anything, whom you hope
can teach you, too, how to do that.

Some renegade botanists
believe the cultivars can be regrown
from even the slightest cutting: one tendril, one stem.
Other experts think this trick can work
for closely related species, but not for them.

V for vigilance. V for vindication.
After a hailstorm, either V in survived,
in visible and invisible. They are the kind
of students who ought to teach, but will not give lectures,
having determined what parts of their own life cycle
are worth trying to explain
to the outer world, what to reveal from within their clusters
of shoots, their extracellular architecture,
and what belongs, for now, on the inside.

Otter Music

They never seem to tire
of each other, nor to tire
each other out, this pair who never bother
with politesse, whose flat paws gather
on each other's shoulders, each the other's
handhold, helpmeet, sous-chef and oyster cracker,
keeping up their noses and their patter,
batting at their whiskered
cheeks, then almost rolling each other over
in the shifting, sometimes swifter
river water. Their triangular
tufts of fur come in ginger
and dirty-snow white as well as in oak-bark colors,
taupe and tea and tan, and grow out denser
than any other mammal's: for such swimmers,
every slip of insulation matters.
If you see them slow, or falter,
less affectionate than their former
selves, never
fault them: tell them winter
is not a thing. Tell them their own river,
the one they do not prefer
so much as call home, will never
wholly freeze over. Tell them that we too gather
in trios, quartets, and pairs; that we shelter
our young. Tell them we too grow older and younger,
that we too are neotenous, that we defer
to the elements reluctantly, though we claim
to stare them down with our big eyes; that their
forepaws are finer
than our oars, that we are the lesser
divers, lesser rowers; that we also whisper,
chatter, splash each other and scream;

that many of us, too, cannot be tamed;
that we plummet when we must. Tell them we admire,
and want to be, rescuers even more
than to be rescued. Tell them we know they would rather
find more time together
than anything. Tell them we feel the same.

James Smith & Sons Umbrellas, Parasols, Etc. (Since 1830)

New Oxford Street

Into some lives a ton of rain must fall.
Our bamboo or wicker or metal
ribs, our tassels, our faux tiger-hide,
our rainbow stripes and overlapping strips
of smooth ultra-waterproof white polyvinyl chloride,
cool to the touch
even after a summer walk,
can't help you then—
not much,
or not at all.
Nor can we propitiate those gods
whose open hand or clenched
fist over clouds and inlets says where and when
and how long and hard it floods.
For life's lesser troubles, however—
too late for lunch, too early
for the residential college ball—
our shade can almost surely
save you from mild folly,
say, from arriving drenched,
as well as from poorly dressed or persistent men.
We may hold hidden spikes, as well
as hardwood handles, posts, and leather straps,
the kind you can swing.
Some of us are adept at all manner of social signaling.
Others are weapons. No one is only one thing.

;

Neither one thing nor the same
thing all the time, I am the punch
lines of jokes about copy and type, the mark of least use,
the maiden aunt of punctuation.
I feel at home in old formes, amid dust and clutter,
akin to the moths whose wings show my outline,
no good in a crunch.
Educated kids forget my name
or try to turn when, if ever, they would choose
me into a game. I am also accused
of harboring ambitions above my station.

I am still figuring some of that out myself.
I know, though, that I was made to join together
things formerly thought incompatible, to be neither-
nor and both-and; to seek a connection
that does not amount to copulation.
In Greek I simply indicate a question.
I always keep one eye open. I know what I've seen.

My siblings-in-arms include the tractor trailer,
platypus, lungfish, merfolk and seaplane.
When challenged about my right
to exist by some precocious reader or editor
who makes my deletion into a helpful suggestion,
I once allowed myself to be struck out;
now, however, I will more likely assert
that I have been around for centuries,
long before anyone asked me to explain.

@#$%^@#!

What's hard is deciding what we need to spell out,
and what would trip you up, where you can't cope.
There is a kind of urban legend, or myth,

that we never say what we mean, or even try,
but those are fighting words. Besides the hype
it's mostly dishonesty we can't stand;

that, and people who have so much self-doubt
that they never say what they want.
Most of us are older than you think.

We definitely do not all have the same type.
Each of us fears isolation, but cherishes solitude,
along with our ability to count,

divide, and let our complex math include
all relevant variables: the x, the y,
and anything else that matters to all of us, with
the important exception of the kitchen
table, or else the kitchen sink.

Poem of 5 a.m.

The fear that you woke up again in your childhood bedroom,
       that your whole adult life was a dream.
There is the plexiglass, or Perspex, case
       guarding the used paperbacks from volume one
to volume nineteen. Volume three was a library loan.
       They make a good team.

Outdoors the flowering plum flips twigs against new leaves
       like thin
collectible coins. One side is a leathery green,
       the other a lighter, more optimistic green.
You pull a bright childhood's lilac-and-white duvet cover
       up to your chin. You are not afraid to be seen.

You're afraid to be seen. The plum tree agrees with your phone:
       they want you to get out of bed. You can get out of bed,
but not yet. Last week or last decade you botched your last-ever
       piano recital by composing an original
fairy tale, silently, in your head,
       about people who lived in a ship in a bottle.

Where did they go? You have memorized every phase
       of cell division: prophase, metaphase, anaphase,
telophase, when new membranes form and part, clean
       as an incision. You turn over,
the beveled duvet-edge pressed to your silent
       lips. You hope nobody asks you
          to make a decision.

Plastic Man Meets Reed Richards in Heaven

Everything seemed to be within your reach:
sex, gadgets, wedding rings, clouds, the roofs of Midtown.
Expert stretcher, gentle landlord, paterfamilias,
best pal of pilots, with a PhD
in confidence, you found an occasion to teach
in every skirmish. Conservation of mass
was never a thing for you, who had it all,
the leading man, the man who understands.

You had my powers. I had no belief
in myself. No wonder I turned myself in
to a chopper, a bedspread, an egg, a red rubber ball,
whatever writers wanted me to be.
Of course I used to be a thief.
Of course I'm always joking. If I meant
what I said, somebody could pin me down.

I remember when there was nothing in my hands.

Love Poem with a Roll on Its Side

What if you really had never heard it before?
The throaty voice, the credibility
And strength of a man who could always pick you up
And bring you to that one place and keep you there
And never abandon you, who would move only slowly
And never in circles, a man who would hold your hand

Gently and yet unrelentingly, whose very
Hairline crept up to a heart-shaped peak
Whose gentle curves matched black-tea-colored eyes
And as-if-penciled brows, so that those farewell-free,
As-long-as-you-need-me tones of reassurance
In him and him alone could be believed. There is so little

On this Earth you can trust, so little that comes around
And never goes away, but we will always
Have this gem, this constant
Companion, this life preserver whose love is a promise
You should have seen coming: he is, indeed, never
Gonna give you up, never gonna let
You down, never gonna run
Around and desert you.

A Deli Counter in Vermont

Your ride home complains   the grocery store is freezing
they'd rather wait outside   The burly guy
with the walrus stache asks whether you want your Italian
with the works   You're not sure what that means

So you ask and he tells you   laboriously surprised
and also do you want tomato   thanks
You lean on the counter and focus   on condensation
the chill on your palm and forearm   and under the glass

the meats in trays and butcher paper beds
(some sausages   sad stacked-up tongue
a leathery souse or loaf)   so out of it

that when he wants to know if that's your order
and calls out loud   Is that your order ma'am
you startle and then apologize   for taking up his time
but he called you ma'am   so you don't mind

Violets in Vermont

together is how they belong

not blades or stalks with leaves not the solitary tall
heads of roses behind the picket
much as we admire their florid order

not the constant sunlight that engenders
eventual drought surely not the repeated
imperative that leads our neighbors to retill a lawn

instead their silver crosshatch and their welcome
interdependence in sunken fields
their narrow roots and their new rain

so gloriously ragged so late to emerge
not so much violet-tinted as lavender-
shaded with slices of blue

a color not in Homer they divide
in order to spread they know how to make
their own beds each morning they make great allies

from each according to soil and wind conditions
to each according to their fragrant needs
the labels mother and father get in the way

for cleistogamous dicots better to say
parent and child rootlet seedling seed
the larger networks on which they rely

spread under wet grass and keep holding one another
their nourished stems like tines of forks and knives
irregularly I know but more than enough
to sustain them Vermont my love for the rest of their lives

Wildflower Meadow, Medawisla

The many-
oared asters
are coracles;

the goldenrod
pods, triremes.
They do not

plan their
voyages
to please us.

The tangle
of brambles
and drupes shifts

only slightly
when the wind
attempts to

part the knee-
or waist-high stalks
and thorns. What will

you do or
be in that state
you fear and look

forward to,
when none of
them need

us, after
the last
seeds leave?

Love Poem with Horticulture and Anxiety

Ever imagine we might be garden gnomes?
      Not the beards or the caps but the aspect of hiding together,
up to our red boots in loamy topsoil, attentive
      to buds in the rain, saying spells that might let them grow stronger,
giving occult encouragement to our ground
      cherries, grape tomatoes on trellises,
pickling cucumbers, wallflowers, helical vines.
      The longer we stand, the more the wooden
soil-boxes feel like palaces,
      the loam itself like food, and like fresh riverbed affines
in which, when sifted, grains of gold are found.
      My love, I am here with you amid the endive,
in the comedy of gardeners who may never
      know what's coming but dig in,
and shade our moderate crops, and do not isolate
      ourselves from regular sun.

Of course we have feet of clay,
      or fins. Of course we made promises—everyone does—
that we will alter together, but not today.
      We cherish our oversize shoes.
Our garden also has sylphs
      that only we can see, and peonies,
and badger tracks, and a sandstone Artemis,
      and colors not found in nature
except in flowerbeds: Intense maroons. Deep golds. Sleek pinks. Warm blues.

Alison Blaire Explains Herself

People get into me,
        I sometimes think,
Not so much for my voice as for all the glitter
        On my belt and sleeves, my dance
Moves, how I swing my hips and hair and see
        Into the crowd amid the phosphorescence,
Or else they dig my adaptability,
        My spangled endurance, my talent for staying alive.
I know how to silence anyone I don't
        Want to hear. I can switch up any sound
Into a light show that can knock you down:
Try to beat me up and I'll turn the beat around.
        I also know my
History: house, complextro,
Metropopolis, escape room, hyperpop.
        I know the moves. I know the repertory.
I wasn't supposed to be white, or straight, or last
        So long. When people cheer
            Me on, I love it, but also I want
            Them to cry
Because they themselves have found love, however
        Much it's a longshot. If I can't
        Keep touring forever, I intend to try.
        My Eighties story
Is always ending. Disco will never die.

Toasty

If, as the self-indulgent sunrise says,
the birds' best day
is the same each day,
then yours is full of news:
sharp textures on dry grass, three kinds of blue
in the shreds of a plastic plaything, and the higher, cooler blue
of this morning. People along our blocks
who still have jobs are clicking the locks
on their front doors, are walking to work,
are bleeping and blooping for you as they unlock
their curbside automobiles. If it sounds to you as Kraftwerk's
Trans-Europe Express or Mahler's Tenth or the most euphoric work-
song would to us, your upright ears
won't help us tell them apart. Robins mating or fighting, the smear
of dried cream cheese along your lower jaw, the ASMR
your paw-clicks make, your shiny nose against an apple core—
everything is yours
to investigate. Everyone watches. Nobody minds.
If you are, as you seem to believe (careful with that door),
our Great Detective, you are the kind
in paperbacks our children used to read, the kind
they ordered from Scholastic based on the covers,
in which a stamp collection left under the cover-
let by an avid younger brother,
a gangly best friend who covers
for him and then gets caught, are the greatest fears
the characters have to handle. The crunch
of a broken branch gave them away. We are here,
you say, sniffing, judging and then approving the air
through the window screen, settling back down on your haunches
in your separate bed, confirming your early hunches.
You are there. I am here. We are here. I know that sound.
For every thing that we have lost or buried
together, another
will be found.

Rambutan

Honestly astonishing
the first time you see them unless you grew up with them,
      they look prickly enough
           to cling to your clothing. Instead

      they are a soft
unsettlement, their promise
      of sweetness more than justified
           inside, like the way

      you told me you once
got to pet a porcupine, nibs
      relaxed and folded back for better
           nuzzling, or the first

      time (after waiting and
waiting) you let me hold
      your hand. Cliché
           means clench, clutch and

      predictable, but also
sometimes true. Sometimes I feel tenderly
      opened up, wet and revealed as if cut
           in two. I want to spend
               today with you.

!

All things must come
to an end, but I never
want them to end: I would rather keep
an open book, continue whatever
gets me excited, replay
a lightning strike, or cast
a plumb line that may never touch
the bottom, crash
through every stubborn wall. It's
true that I come to a point. I divide
each present from every past. But I also exist
to celebrate what's next; I support
purposiveness, enterprise, and the intrepid spirit
of getting things done. That's why I feel deeply akin
to vacuum cleaners, to the letter T,
to batteries, and to the short
and long versions of any handmade stroke
that could be the numeral 1, or an l, or an I.
I am, also, an inkblot, a sudden stain
emerging below a quill pen, a sign
of danger, and a way to be overjoyed,
an antiquated firearm along
with smoke from its retort.
And I have been able to see
myself as a telescope;
a way to print
the otherwise
unprintable; a tail
for flight, or for seaside escape,
and even the kind
of anchor that stands for hope.
I am the lever big enough
to move the world, the world you move,

actions and actors,
the proof and the claim you prove,
the product of all mathematical factors.
You cannot use me
as a taxi, or for a quick lift, or just to get
yourself from one place to another; I mean to stay.
I can announce
the end of everything,
the feeling of dangling, of having
the world on a string,
or else a new day.

We Are Mermaids Again

Eyes on the distance, past
the last
homes that remain
above the tideline on the coastal plain,
we listen for the overlap of salt
spray with the laminar
flow underneath. Sun changes everything, this far south.

Nothing for it, this far into our future,
except to be the mermaids, and welcome any
visitor who can help maintain
our underwater villages, carved from basalt
and sediment, full
of chill
ladders and handholds, indigo-gray, with canes

of coral, and broad pillars, and childcare
in reinforced bubbles, with painted tails for charm,
and teachers, and town meetings, a kelp farm,

and mazes for children to swim through, and orature,
melodious, easily memorized, and anemones
exploring their territories, on the wet flats,
and the soft gardens and quadrats
on the low terrain about the harbor mouth.

Ligature

Binary thinking leaves out so much. For example,
Reading only left to right, or up and down,

Ignores all our wishes for comfort, for circular motion,
All the ways that the happier letterforms seek the option

Not to stand alone. Their living space is ample,
Hot in June, cold in March, with pencil lines of frost

Along the stems and twigs in all their dewy, new-built
Nests. Some warblers build more than one.

Each feels tiny compared to thunderstorms, construction
Cranes, plate tectonics and how the past

Harms the present with its slush-avalanches of guilt,
And yet it made us—us. How little we know. How much

Knowing isn't the point. We love how the letters can touch.

ACKNOWLEDGMENTS

Many thanks to these periodicals, anthologies, and online events, and to their editors, for publishing and sponsoring poems in this volume, sometimes in different forms or under different names:

The Academy of American Poets' *Poem-a-Day*: "A Deli Counter in Vermont"; *Anthropocene*: "Turkeys in Harvard Yard"; *BackSTORY* "Some Like It Hot"; Bad Lilies: "We are Mermaids," "Alison Blaire Explains Herself," "Plastic Man Meets Reed Richards in Heaven"; *Boston Hassle*: "Love Poem with Major Appliance"; *Boston Review*: "Boeing 757s, Airbus 320s, an Embraer 190"; *Food & Wine*: "At the Parkway Deli"; *FUSION*: "Before the Wedding," "Introduction to Trans Literature," "Song of Kate the Pirate Queen"; *Hampden Sydney Poetry Review*: "—," "!," "( )," "" "," ";," "@#$%^@#!"; *Harvard Advocate*: "" ""; *Harvard Review*: "Wildflower Meadow, Medawisla"; *Landfall*: "Kite Day, New Brighton"; *The Literary Review* (NJ): "Snow"; *London Review of Books*: "Potomac River, 1982," "Rambutan," "Sparrows in the Natick Collection"; *Marsh Hawk Review*: "Rain," "Whiter"; *Michigan Quarterly Review*: "Cinderella"; *Moist*: "Love Poem with Comic Books on Saturdays"; National Public Radio/*All Things Considered*: "Love Poem with Horticulture and Anxiety"; *The New Yorker*: "Lamb's Ear"; *Pangyrus*: "Civilization"; *Pericles at Play*: "Two Shields"; *Plume*: "Bleeding Hearts," "Impatiens," "Cabbage Whites"; *Poetry*: "Love Poem with Archery"; *The Poetry Review* (UK): "Toasty"; *Raritan*: "James Smith & Sons Umbrellas, Parasols, Etc. (Since 1830)," "Prayer for Werewolves"; *Salamander*: "Love Poem with a Roll on Its Side," "Miami"; *Scoundrel Time*: "My 1993," "My 1994," "Geysers"; *Turbine/Kapohau*: "Whale Watch"

All We Know of Pleasure: Poetic Erotica by Women, ed. Enid Shomer (Durham, NC: Carolina Wren, 2019): "Love Poem with Summer Camp Reunion"

Together in a Sudden Strangeness: America's Poets Respond to the Pandemic, ed. Alice Quinn (New York, NY: Knopf, 2020): "Love Poem with Major Appliance"

My thanks also to *Abridged*, *Aotearotica*, *ComicsXF*, *The Guardian*, *Hilobrow*, *Hopkins Review*, *The Kenyon Review*, *Literary Imagination*, *The Poetry Brothel*

Anthology, *Strange Horizons*, and *Words and Music at the Skep*, and to their editors and organizers, for sharing, supporting, and publishing poems completed during the writing of this volume but not included here.

Several poems from part two of this volume also appeared in *For All Mutants: A Chapbook with Heroes* (Minneapolis, MN: Rain Taxi, 2021). I'm especially grateful to Eric Lorberer, Kelly Everding, and all involved with the production of that chapbook.

The people at Graywolf are, of course, irreplaceable and amazing. Let's keep doing this for a while. Extra thanks here to Jeff Shotts.

Thanks also to my colleagues at Harvard and at the University of Canterbury in Christchurch, New Zealand, for letting me work alongside them, and especially to the chairs: Glenda Carpio, James Engel, Paul Millar, James Simpson, and Nicholas Watson. Vivid thanks to Nicholas Nace, without whom no punctuation is safe. Inexhaustible thanks, as well, to my students and former students, who keep on reading with me.

"" "" is for Cat Fitzpatrick. "Boeing 757s, Airbus 320s, an Embraer 190," "Love Poem with Comic Books on Saturdays," "Love Poem with Summer Camp Reunion," and "!" are for Rachel Gold. "My 1993" comes from an idea by Sophie Szew. "My 1994" is for my summer 2021 students and after Brenda Shaughnessy. "Hobbies" is for Monica Youn. "Rambutan" is for Mara Hampson. "Before the Wedding" is for Katyana. "Prayer for Werewolves" is for Rahne Sinclair. "Kurt Wagner's Song" is for Anna Peppard. "Love Poem with Major Appliance," "Violets in Vermont," and "Love Poem with Horticulture and Anxiety" are for Jessica Bennett. "Plastic Man Meets Reed Richards in Heaven" is for Douglas Wolk. "We Are Mermaids Again" is for Fiona Hopkins. "Ligature" is for Brian Hanechak.

More than ever I am aware of how many people have helped me over the years in which these poems came into being, and of many people I rely on today. I am especially happy to have in my life—and to see in some of these poems, directly or otherwise—Rae Armantrout, Sandra Beasley, Jessica Bennett, Sandra and

Jeffrey Burt, Callie Davis, Jordan Ellenberg, Eowyn Evans, Cat Fitzpatrick, Kate Fractal, Forrest Gander, Maia Gemmill, Carmen Giménez, Rachel Gold, Jorie Graham, Mara Hampson, Karen Healey, Brian Hanechak, Fiona Hopkins, Laura Kasischke, Ariel Landau, Hilary Lerner, Matt McGowan, Paul Muldoon, Misha Petryk, Catherine Rockwood, Zach Schrag, Annie Staats, Rachel Trousdale, Rebecca Tushnet, Helen Vendler, verity, Douglas Wolk, Monica Youn, and, of course, Nathan and Cooper Bennett Burt, who may or may not see themselves in these pages but take center stage in our shared lives.

STEPHANIE BURT is Professor of English at Harvard. Her books of poetry and literary criticism include *After Callimachus* (Princeton University Press, 2020); *Don't Read Poetry: A Book about How to Read Poems* (Basic, 2019); *Advice from the Lights* (Graywolf, 2017), a National Endowment for the Arts Big Read selection; *The Poem Is You: 60 Contemporary American Poems and How to Read Them* (Harvard University Press, 2016); *Belmont* (Graywolf, 2013); and *Close Calls with Nonsense: Reading New Poetry* (Graywolf, 2009), a National Book Critics Circle Award finalist. Her writing on poems, poets, poetry, science fiction, superheroes, comic books, pop music, LGBTQ+ existence, and transgender joy has appeared in *American Literary History, ComicsXF, London Review of Books*, the *New York Times Book Review*, the *New Yorker, Rain Taxi*, the *Times Literary Supplement*, the *Yale Review*, and other journals in the United States, Canada, Ireland, the United Kingdom, and New Zealand. She lives in Belmont, Massachusetts, with her spouse and nesting partner Jessica Bennett, two children, two cats, one very sweet rescue dog, many loveys, a lot of X-Men comics, and a few dozen polyhedral dice.

The text of *We Are Mermaids* is set in Granjon LT Std.
Book design by Rachel Holscher.
Composition by Bookmobile Design and Digital
Publisher Services, Minneapolis, Minnesota.
Manufactured by Versa Press on acid-free,
30 percent postconsumer wastepaper.